W9-BQS-981

Cosmos Chronicles
Spectacular
Space Stations

Elsie Olson

Lerner Publications ◆ Minneapolis

Lerner Publications Company
A division of Lerner Publishing Group, Inc.
241 First Avenue North
Minneapolis, MN 55401 USA

For reading levels and more information, look up this title at www.lernerbooks.com.

Main body text set in Caecilia LT Std 11.25/20
Typeface provided by Adobe Systems.

Photo Acknowledgements
The images in this book are used with permission of: © NASA/Crew of STS-132/Wikimedia Commons, pp. 4–5; © Wikimedia Commons, p. 5; © NASA, pp. 6, 8, 9 (ISS), 14, 15 (top), 17 (bottom), 18, 21 (top), 24, 25 (top, middle, bottom), 26, 27 (top, middle), 29; © Amanda Slater/Flickr, p. 7 (bottom); © Roger Ressmeyer/Corbis/VCG/Getty Images, p. 7 (top); © NASA On the Commons/Flickr, pp. 9 (bottom), 12, 13 (top), 20, 21 (bottom), 22; © NASA/Wikimedia Commons, pp. 9 (Skylab), 9 (Mir), 10, 11 (top), 13 (bottom), 15 (bottom), 19 (top, bottom), 27 (bottom); © SVF2/Getty Images, p. 9 (Salyut); © Xinhua News Agency/Getty Images, p. 9 (Tiangong); © NASA Johnson/Flickr, pp. 11 (bottom), 23; © NASA/Bill Stafford/Wikimedia Commons, p. 16; © Copyright Airbus, p. 17 (top); © NASA/Bill Ingalls/Wikimedia Commons, p. 28

Cover: © NASA
Design elements: © NASA/JPL-Caltech/STScI/IRAM

Library of Congress Cataloging-in-Publication Data

The Cataloging-in-Publication Data for *Spectacular Space Stations* is on file at the Library of Congress.
ISBN 978-1-5415-5597-6 (lib. bdg.)
ISBN 978-1-5415-7371-0 (pbk.)
ISBN 978-1-5415-5645-4 (eb pdf)

Manufactured in the United States of America
1 – CG – 7/15/19

Contents

A New Frontier

Throughout history, humans have tested the limits of survival on Earth. Now humans are pushing to survive in outer space!

With **microgravity**, extreme temperatures, and no oxygen, space is the most challenging **environment** yet. Staying alive in these conditions might sound like science fiction. And yet, since the 1970s, select groups of humans have called space home. These bold explorers stay in **orbiting** outposts called space stations.

Space stations are human-made structures sent into Earth's orbit. They allow humans to live in space for long periods of time. Some explorers have lived in space for over a year at a time!

CAN YOU SPOT THE ISS?

The International Space Station (ISS) orbits Earth every ninety minutes. On a clear night, the bright space station can be seen with the naked eye. Want to see when the ISS is flying above your house? Check out spotthestation.nasa.gov.

As of 2018, only one space station was permanently **inhabited**. It is the International Space Station (ISS).

The Skylab crew practiced the repair underwater before trying it in space.

NASA's Daring Space Repair

On May 14, 1973, NASA launched its first space station, Skylab. It was a laboratory where people could perform science experiments in space. Skylab launched separate from the crew.

However, Skylab ran into trouble during launch. A shield meant to protect it from the sun's extreme heat was torn off. So, while Skylab went into orbit, NASA delayed the crew's launch to plan a repair.

On May 25, the crew launched and met up with Skylab. The team added a new solar shield while **tethered** to Skylab. It was the most complex repair ever done in space! Skylab went on to host several crews of astronauts.

SKYLAB BACKSTORY

Skylab was a first for NASA, but the Soviet Union built the first space station. Salyut 1 launched in 1971.

SKYLAB CRASHES IN AUSTRALIA

In 1979, an empty Skylab came crashing back to Earth. Pieces of the station landed in western Australia. No one was injured. But an Australian town fined the United States $400 for littering.

In 1979, a spaceship **crashed** over Esperance. We fined them $400 for **littering**.

Esperance Out of the way. Out of this world. australiasgoldenoutback.com visitesperance.com

7

All Aboard the ISS

The ISS orbits Earth at 17,500 miles (28,164 km) per hour! The station is the result of a **collaboration** between the United States, Russia, and many other countries to build an orbiting laboratory.

The ISS has operated continuously since 2000 and will likely stay in orbit until the 2020s. It can hold up to ten people. ISS crewmembers conduct research and scientific experiments to better understand what living in space does to the human body.

SPACE STATIONS THROUGHOUT HISTORY: HUMAN OCCUPATION

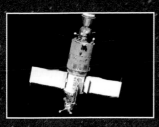

1971–1986
Salyut 1-7
(Russia)

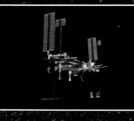

2000–Present
International
Space Station
(Russia,
United States,
European Space
Agency, Canada,
Japan)

1973–1974
Skylab (United
States)

1986–2000
Mir (Soviet
Union/Russia)

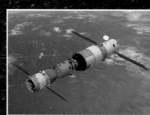

2011–2013
Tiangong-1
(China)

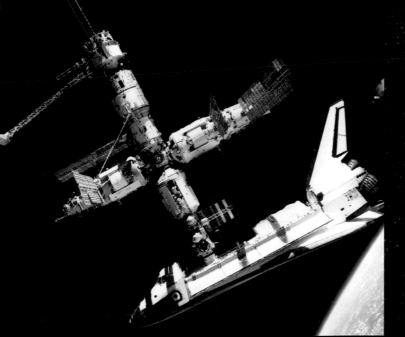

ISS BACKSTORY: MIR

Mir was Russia's longest-lasting space station. It helped pave the way for the ISS. Mir held a crew of six that later included US astronauts. In 2001, Mir was brought back to Earth.

Piece by Piece: Construction in Orbit

The ISS weighs 925,000 pounds (419,573 kg). It is as long as a football field and has more living space than a five-bedroom house!

A rocket would not be powerful enough to launch a station of this size. So NASA and its international partners assembled each piece of the station in space.

The ISS is made of more than one hundred parts. The first piece was launched in 1998. The final piece was added in 2011. But new capsules, called modules, continue to be added.

ROBOTIC ARM HELPS BUILD ISS

In 2001, robotic arm Canadarm2 was **installed** on the ISS to help build the rest of the station. Astronauts controlled the limb from inside the ISS. Today, this arm helps astronauts do work on **spacewalks**.

EXTRATERRESTRIAL OPINION

"It's like building a ship in the middle of the ocean from the keel up. . . You've got to float and you've got to sail. All this has to occur while you're actually building the ship, and that's what station is like."

— Mike Suffredini, NASA station program manager, describing construction of the ISS

Inside Look: The Anatomy of a Space Station

The ISS is divided into two main parts. The Russian side is where **cosmonauts** live and work. The US side is where US, Canadian, European, and Japanese astronauts live and work. Within each side are smaller areas, called modules. These hold living quarters, laboratories, and work spaces.

Smaller capsules, called nodes, link the modules together. Docking ports around the ISS allow spacecraft to attach to the station to deliver supplies or crewmembers. Solar panels provide power to the station.

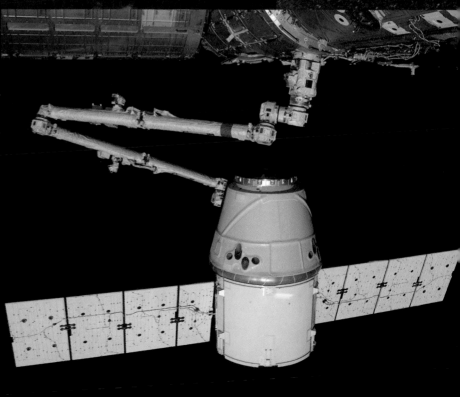

GETTING THERE

It takes six hours to reach the ISS from Earth. Crewmembers arrive on a Russian Soyuz spacecraft. A Soyuz stays docked on the ISS at all times so the crew can escape in case of an emergency aboard the station.

DRAGON BREAKS NEW BARRIERS

In 2012, the first private spacecraft docked at the ISS. Private space company SpaceX built the craft, called Dragon. Dragon continues to deliver cargo to and from the station.

The ISS mission control center on Earth

Earthlings Control the ISS!

Much of the ISS is controlled from the ground. Mission control centers around the world operate the station and plan nearly every part of an ISS astronaut's day.

NASA's mission control is in Houston, Texas. It is staffed twenty-four hours a day, 365 days a year. All other ISS mission control centers communicate with Houston.

AMES

GRC

HQ

MSFC

JSC

NASA CONTROL CENTERS

NASA Headquarters (HQ), Washington, DC
Oversees the ISS program

**Johnson Space Center
(JSC), Houston Texas**
Operates the US modules from the ground
and coordinates with international partners

**Marshall Space Flight Center
(MSFC), Huntsville, Alabama**
Controls experiments done on the ISS

**Telescience Support Centers:
MSFC; JSC; Moffet Field, California
(AMES); Cleveland, Ohio (GRC)**
Provide support for science experiments
aboard ISS

IS THERE WI-FI
IN SPACE?

ISS astronauts can
communicate with mission
control, family, and friends from
space thanks to the internet.
Astronauts email, video chat,
and use social media to keep in
touch with earthlings.

Space Station Boot Camp Lasts Years

ISS astronauts are chosen out of tens of thousands of **applicants**. Then they undergo two years of training! Language studies is part of training. All ISS crewmembers must speak English to communicate with mission control and Russian to communicate with transport control.

ISS trainees also learn how to use ISS technology. They practice missions at the bottom of a pool. Working in a spacesuit underwater is similar to the conditions astronauts experience on spacewalks.

FLOATING ROBOT JOINS ISS CREW

In 2018, SpaceX's Dragon spacecraft brought the first robot crewmember to the ISS. The round robot's name was CIMON. It was programmed to help complete several tasks.

ASTRONAUT DIARIES

ISS astronauts often keep journals about their experiences on the ISS. These are published on NASA's website.

Recycling Sweat, Urine, and Bathwater

Water is heavy and expensive to ship to space. So every drop of water aboard the ISS is recycled. Systems capture water from urine, sweat, showers, and even the moisture in the astronauts' breath! The water is filtered and treated. Astronauts use it for drinking, cooking, and cleaning.

VACUUM TOILETS SUCK WASTE

Using the bathroom isn't easy on the ISS. Astronauts strap themselves to the toilet so they don't float away! Then they attach a **suction** device to their bodies. The device works like a vacuum and sucks waste away.

EATING AND HEATING FLOATING FOOD

The ISS has an oven so astronauts can heat up food. But there is no refrigerator, so they eat non-perishable foods. Astronauts must eat tidily. Crumbs that float away can clog air vents!

An observatory module on the ISS

A Day in the Life of an ISS Astronaut

ISS astronauts typically wake at 7:00 a.m. They eat breakfast and have a meeting with mission control to discuss daily tasks. Some tasks are exciting, like spacewalks. Others are less glamorous, like emptying urine containers.

The astronauts usually work until about 6:00 p.m. Then they have another mission control meeting and eat dinner. The astronauts have free time until bedtime. Many spend this time exercising, watching movies, and taking in the views of space.

WHAT TO WEAR?

Imagine wearing the same underwear for four days. Some ISS astronauts do just that! There's no washing machine on the ISS, so astronauts throw away their clothes after wearing them. They first try to get as much use out of the items as possible.

TAKING OUT SPACE TRASH

ISS astronauts store garbage in a cargo vessel. When the vessel is full, they launch it back toward Earth. The vessel and garbage burn up in Earth's atmosphere.

Complex Prep for Strolls in Space

A spacewalk takes hours of preparation. Astronauts don't go on them just for fun. They usually go to make repairs to the station or perform science experiments.

SUITING UP FOR SPACE

Most spacewalk preparation is spent getting the astronaut's body used to lower air pressure inside the spacesuit. If an astronaut's body isn't given time to adjust, she could die.

24 hours pre-walk: ISS cabin pressure is reduced, and the oxygen level is increased.

2 hours and 20 minutes pre-walk: Astronaut enters the airlock and breathes pure oxygen for at least 60 minutes. Next, the airlock is depressurized. The astronaut then begins putting on the spacesuit.

1 hour pre-walk: The pressure inside the airlock is reduced to match the pressure inside the spacesuit.

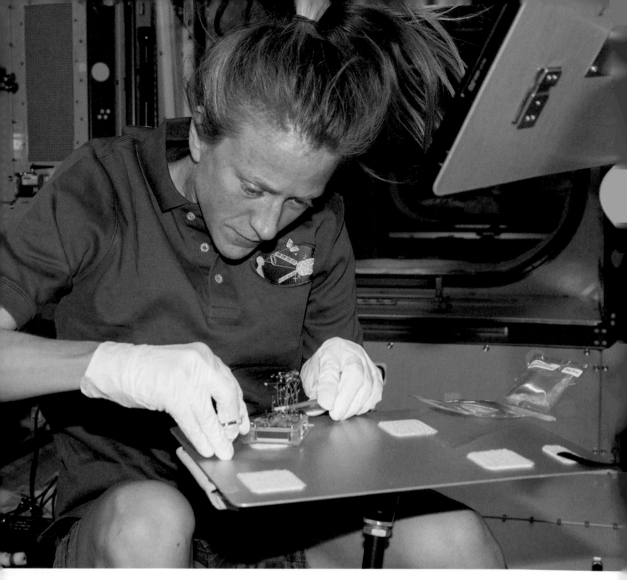

Astronauts Perform Experiments in Midair

Astronauts aboard the ISS are there to do research. In one mission, astronauts might do 300 different experiments! These experiments include studying ways to survive in space long-term, growing plants in space, and more.

From Space Plants to Cosmic Fire: ISS Experiments

SPACE GARDEN

Objective: Set up a space garden with a variety of plant species to provide fresh food that can be grown and eaten in space.

TWINS STUDY

Objective: Compare **identical** twin astronauts Scott and Mark Kelly after Scott had been aboard ISS for about one year. This let NASA see how microgravity can change the human body.

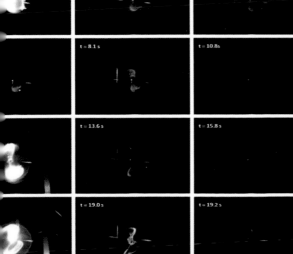

t = 8.1 s t = 10.8 s

t = 13.6 s t = 15.8 s

t = 19.0 s t = 19.2 s

SPACE FLAMES

Objective: Study how fire burns in microgravity.

Space Crews Face Constant Cosmic Dangers

Astronauts face danger every day just by being in space! Microgravity causes slight loss of bone and muscle mass. It can cause vision problems too. However, most of these risks aren't life-threatening during short missions. But other dangers could equal disaster on the ISS.

WHAT IF A FIRE STARTS IN SPACE?

A fire would quickly travel through the ISS if not contained and put out. On the US side of the station, astronauts use CO2 to put out fires. On the Russian side, cosmonauts use soapy water.

DEPRESSURIZATION IS POSSIBLE

Depressurization means the ISS is leaking air. This might happen if a meteoroid hits and punctures the station. Astronauts must abandon the ISS if they cannot quickly find and stop a leak.

TOXIC SPILLS COULD KILL

The ISS uses **ammonia** to cool its electronics. Breathing ammonia can cause nose and throat damage, blindness, and death. If ammonia leaks in the ISS, astronauts must evacuate.

Cosmos Exclusive!

What's new and upcoming in space station technology?

Inflatable Space Stations Coming Soon?

Private US company Bigelow Aerospace is developing an **inflatable** space habitat. Space station parts can only be as large as the rocket carrying them into space. Inflatable parts would be deflated and small while being carried up. In space, they could be inflated to become much larger!

Russia Talks Space Hotel

Russia's space agency has discussed adding a luxury hotel room to the ISS. Tourists could stay in this room, but it would cost a lot. A trip starts at around $40 million!

Space Gets a Garbage Truck

Earth is surrounded by **space junk**. Space junk can be dangerous for orbiting space stations. In 2018, ISS astronauts began testing a satellite made to collect space junk. It uses a net, drag sail, and **harpoon** to catch the debris.

What's Next for the ISS?

ISS is set to be decommissioned in the 2020s. Then, some of its parts may be reused in future space stations. But much of the ISS will crash to a watery grave in the Pacific Ocean.

Glossary

ammonia: a strong-smelling chemical used in cleaning products

applicants: people who apply for something

collaboration: the action of working with others to do something

cosmonauts: Russian astronauts

environment: the surrounding circumstances or conditions

harpoon: a long spear with an attached rope that can be shot from a special gun

identical: exactly the same

inflatable: able to be filled with air

inhabited: lived in

installed: put into a place where it can be used

microgravity: the near-absence of gravity in space

orbiting: traveling in a circular path around something, especially a planet or the sun

space junk: old satellites and other human-made debris as well as natural objects, such as meteoroids

spacewalk: a period of activity spent outside a spacecraft by an astronaut in space

suction: the act of drawing air out of a space

tethered: roped or chained to something

Further Information

BOOKS

Cardell, Eleanor. *Liftoff! Space Exploration*. Minneapolis: Lerner Publications, 2018.
Discover the history of space exploration and how it impacted the world.

Goldstein, Margaret J. *Astronauts: A Space Discovery Guide*. Minneapolis: Lerner Publications, 2017.
Read all about astronauts' work, research, and challenges in space.

Richmond, Benjamin. *Life in Space: Beyond Planet Earth*. New York: Sterling, 2018.
Explore what it's like to live on the International Space Station!

WEBSITES

ESA Kids—The International Space Station
https://www.esa.int/esaKIDSen/SEMZXJWJD1E_LifeinSpace_0.html
Discover more about space stations with cool photos and articles from the ESA.

JAXA—Space Station Kids!
http://iss.jaxa.jp/kids/en/
Check out facts, photos, and more on the Japan Aerospace Exploration Agency's space stations site.

Our Universe for Kids—International Space Station
https://www.ouruniverseforkids.com/iss-international-space-station/
Find fun facts about the ISS and a video exploring its different modules.

Index